HAL•LEONARD

PIANO PLAY-ALONG

PIANO | VOCAL | GUITAR ■ CD

VOLUME 77

ELTON JOHN
FAVORITES

T0085045

ISBN 978-1-4234-7990-1

HAL•LEONARD®
CORPORATION
7777 W. BLUEMOUND RD. P.O. BOX 13819 MILWAUKEE, WI 53213

Visit Hal Leonard Online at
www.halleonard.com

CONTENTS

BENNIE AND THE JETS

Words and Music by ELTON JOHN
and BERNIE TAUPIN

Hey kids __ shake __ it loose to-geth-er the spot-light's hit-ting some thing that's been known to change the weath-er.
Hey kids __ plug __ in-to the faith-less may-be they're __ blind-ed but Ben-nie makes them age-less.
Solo ad lib.

-nie she's_ real-ly keen, she's got e-lec-tric boots a mo-hair suit_ you know I

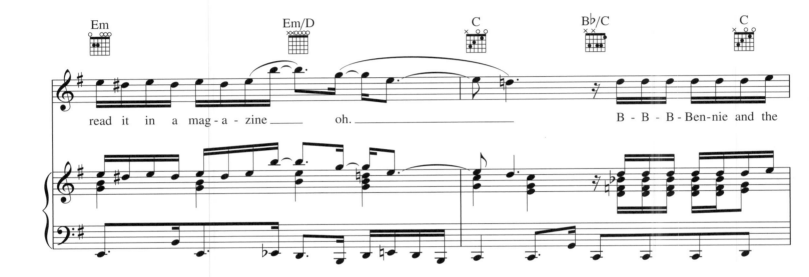

read it in a mag-a-zine_____ oh._____ B - B - B - Ben-nie and the

Jets.

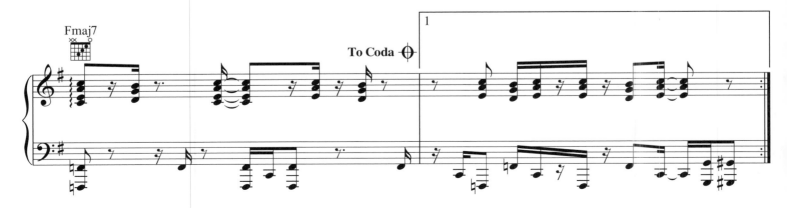

To Coda

1

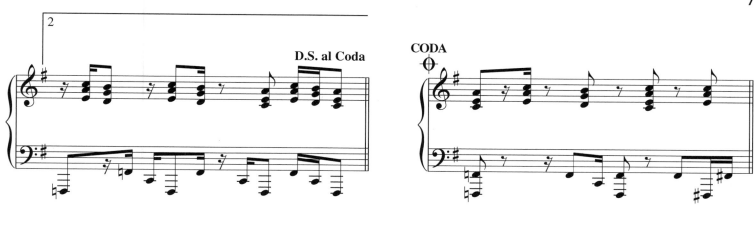

Ben-nie Ben-nie Ben-nie Ben-nie and the Jets. _____

BLUE EYES

Words and Music by ELTON JOHN
and GARY OSBORNE

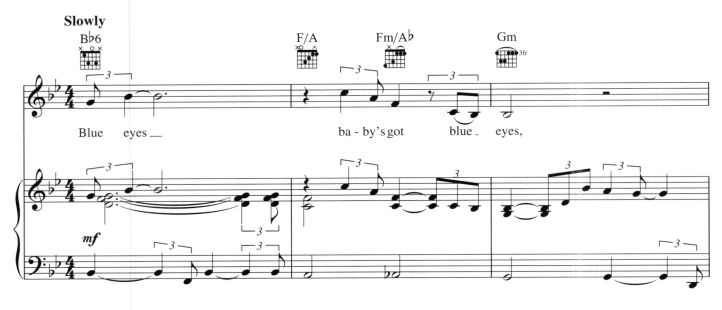

Blue eyes ___ ba-by's got blue ___ eyes,

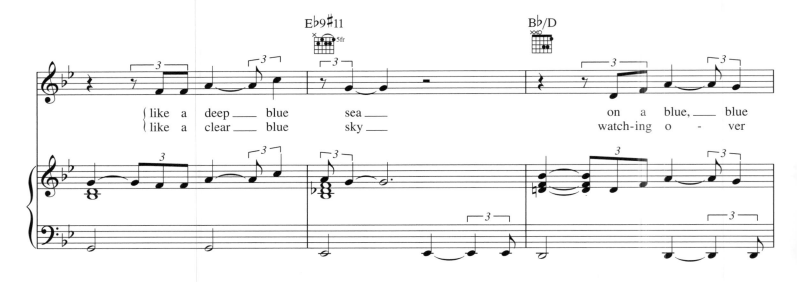

{ like a deep ___ blue sea ___ on a blue, ___ blue
{ like a clear ___ blue sky ___ watch-ing o - ver

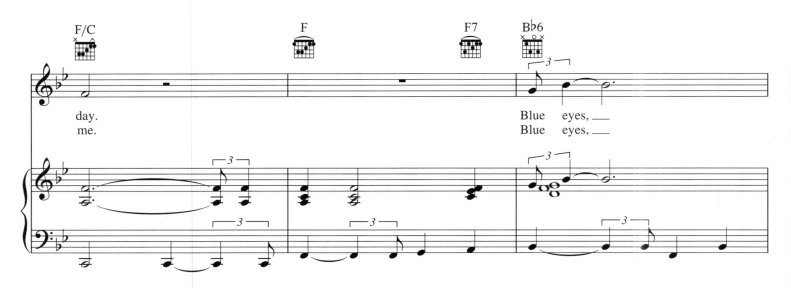

day.
me.

Blue eyes, ___
Blue eyes, ___

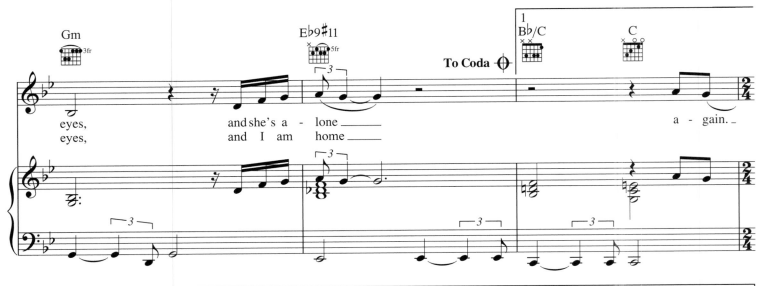

eyes, and she's a - lone _____
eyes, and I am home _____

a - gain. _

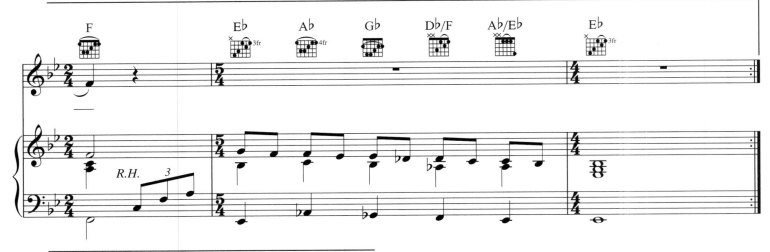

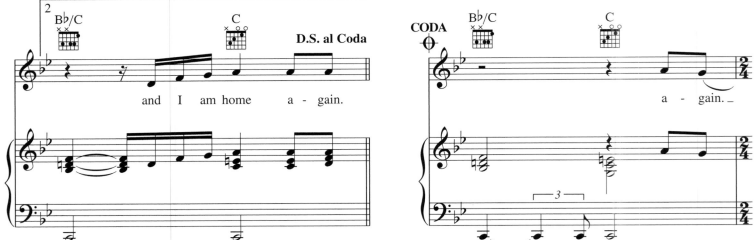

and I am home a - gain.

a - gain. _

DON'T GO BREAKING MY HEART

Words and Music by CARTE BLANCHE
and ANN ORSON

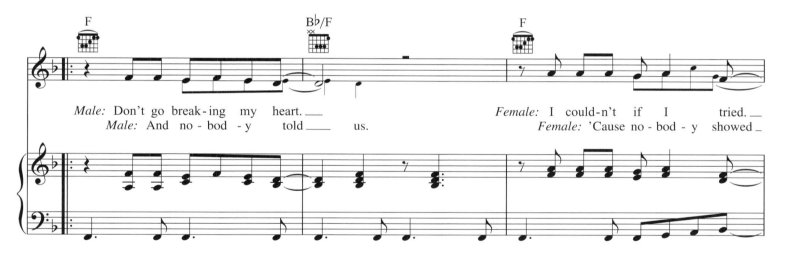

Male: Don't go break-ing my heart. ___ *Female:* I could-n't if I tried. ___
Male: And no-bod-y told ___ us. *Female:* 'Cause no-bod-y showed ___

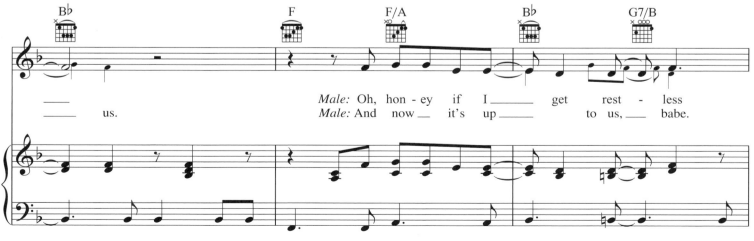

___ us. *Male:* Oh, hon-ey if I ___ get rest-less
Male: And now ___ it's up ___ to us, ___ babe.

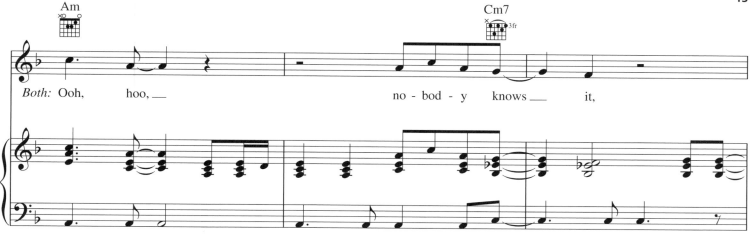

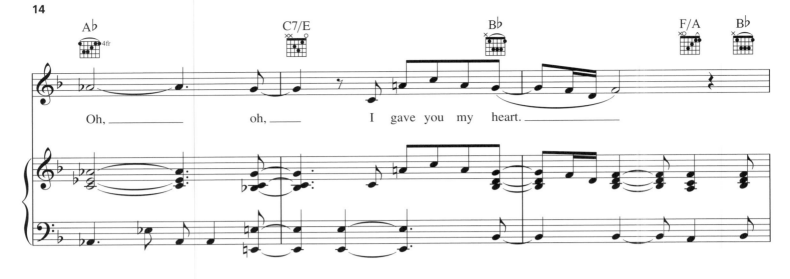

Oh, _____ oh, _____ I gave you my heart. _____

Male: So, don't go break-ing my heart. _____

To Coda ⊕

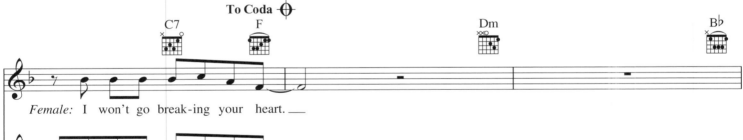

Female: I won't go break-ing your heart. ___

Both: Don't go break-ing my heart. ___

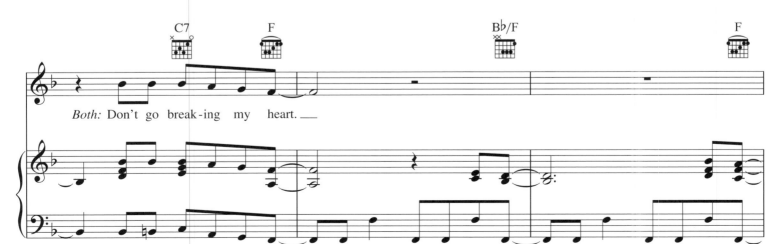

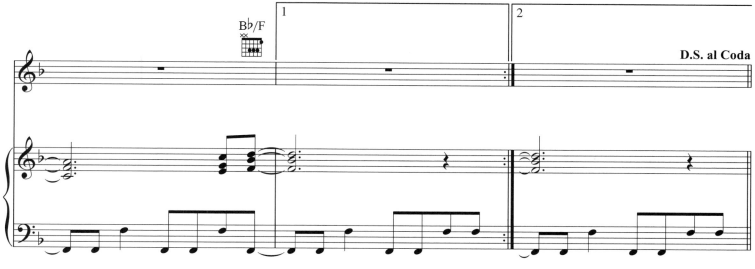

D.S. al Coda

CODA

Both:
Don't go break-ing my don't go break-ing my don't go break-ing my heart.

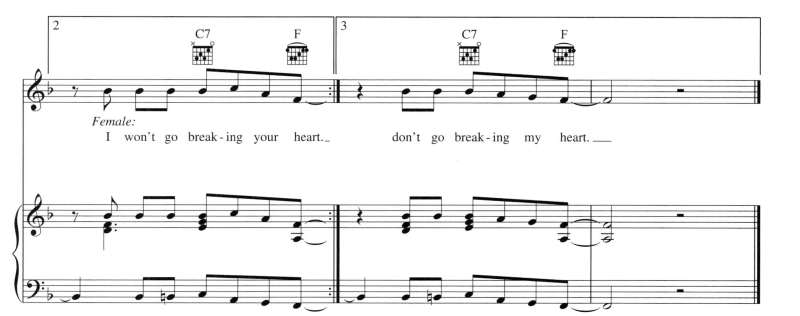

Female:
I won't go break-ing your heart. don't go break-ing my heart.

ROCKET MAN
(I Think It's Gonna Be a Long Long Time)

Words and Music by ELTON JOHN
and BERNIE TAUPIN

Moderately slow, with a beat

then.

I miss__ the earth__ so much,__ I miss my wife,____

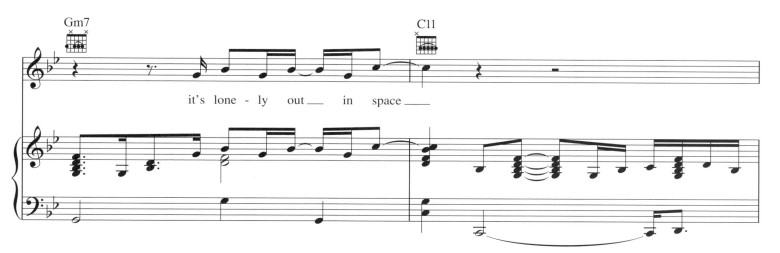

it's lone-ly out__ in space____

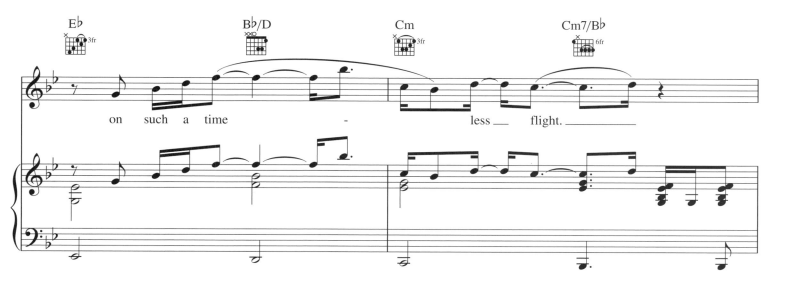

on such a time - less__ flight.____

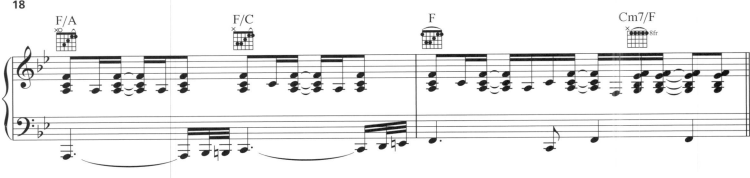

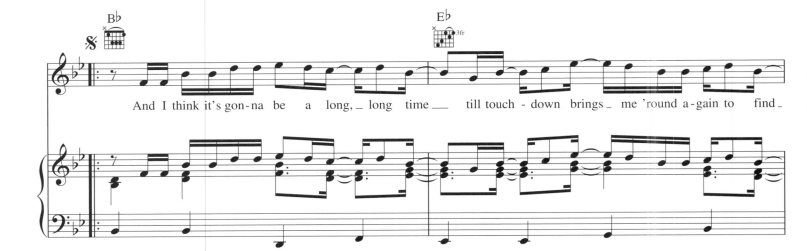

And I think it's gon-na be a long,__ long time__ till touch-down brings__ me 'round a-gain to find__

__ I'm not the man__ they think I am at home,__ oh no__ no no,__ I'm a

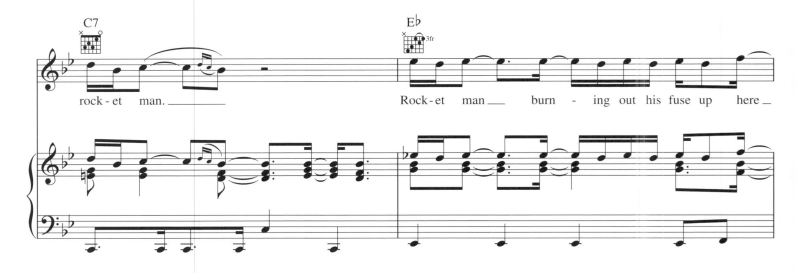

rock-et man._____ Rock-et man__ burn-ing out his fuse up here__

them   if you did.

And all ___ this sci - ence ___   I don't

un - der - stand.   It's just ___ my job ___ five days a week. ___

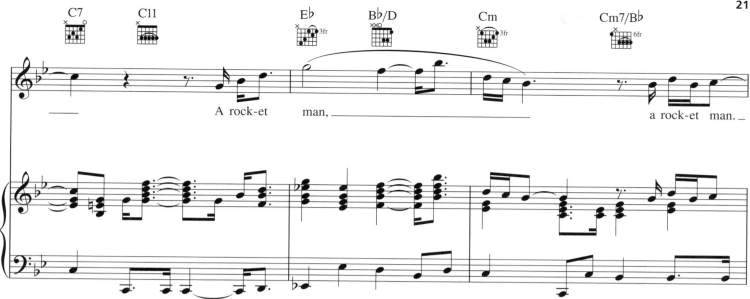

A rock-et man, _____ a rock-et man. _

D.S. al Coda

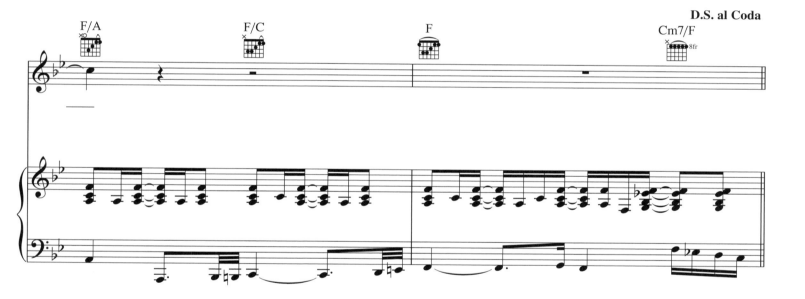

CODA

Repeat and Fade

And I think it's gon-na be a long, __ long time. __

SACRIFICE

Words and Music by ELTON JOHN
and BERNIE TAUPIN

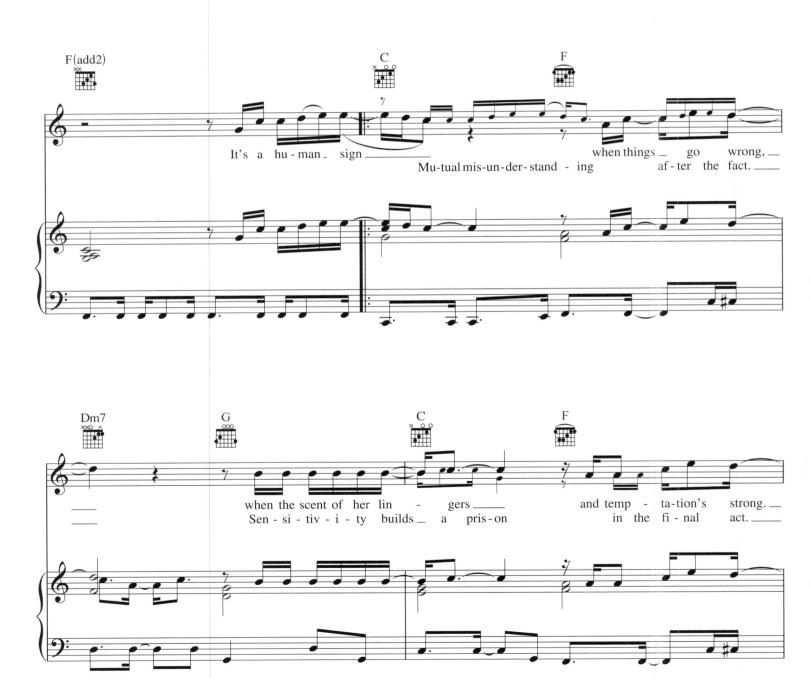

Recorded a half step higher.

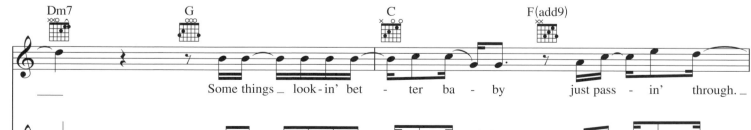

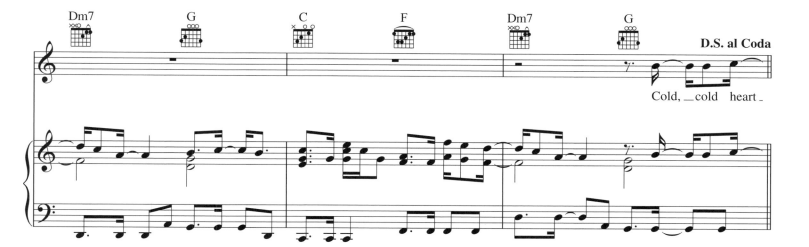

Cold, __cold heart __

No sac - ri - fice _____ at all.

No sac - ri - fice _____ at all.

SOMEONE SAVED MY LIFE TONIGHT

Words and Music by ELTON JOHN
and BERNIE TAUPIN

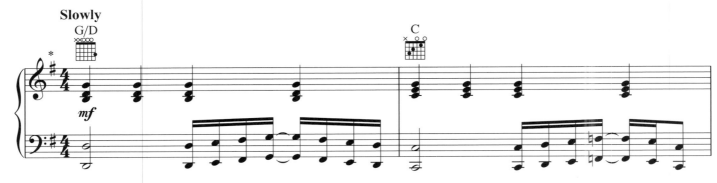

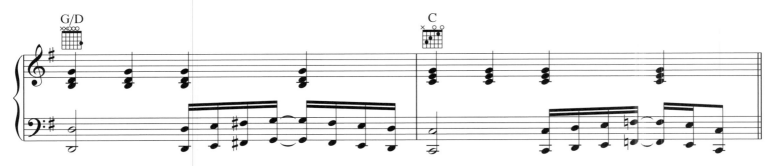

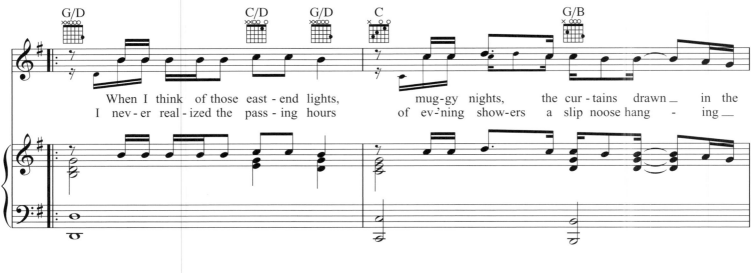

When I think of those east-end lights, mug-gy nights, the cur-tains drawn in the
I nev-er real-ized the pass-ing hours of ev'-ning show-ers a slip noose hang - ing

lit - tle room down - stairs, I'm
in my dark - est dreams. I'm

* *Recorded a half step higher.*

pri - ma don - na, lord, you real-ly should have been there, _ sit-ting like a prin-cess perched _ in her e-lec-
stran-gled by your haunt - ed so - cial scene, _ just a _ pawn _ out-played _ by a dom i -nat-

- tric chair. _ And it's one more beer, _ and I don't hear you
- ing queen. _ It's four o' - clock _ in the morn-ing damn it!

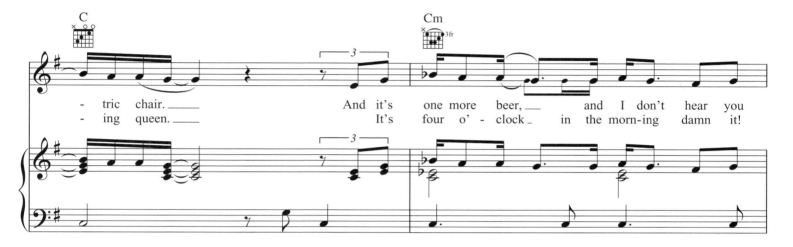

an - y - more. _ We've all _ gone cra - zy late - ly, my
Lis - ten to _ me good. _ I'm _ sleep - ing with my - self _ to - night

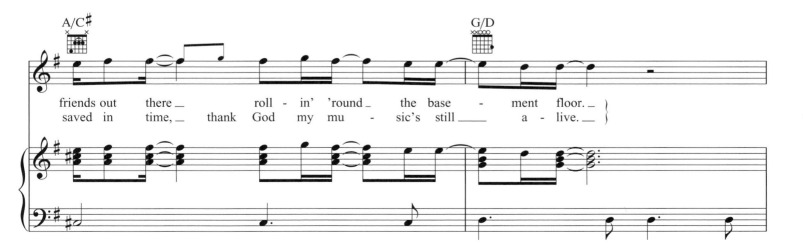

friends out there _ roll - in' 'round _ the base - ment floor. _
saved in time, _ thank God my mu - sic's still _ a - live. _

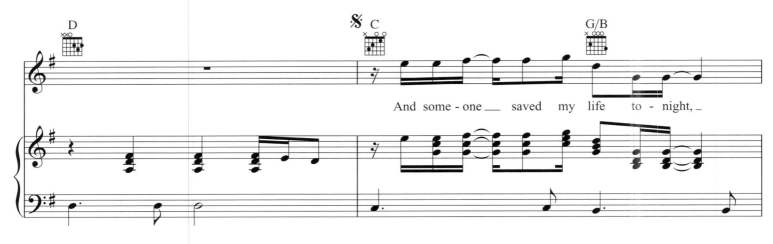

And some-one ___ saved my life to - night, ___

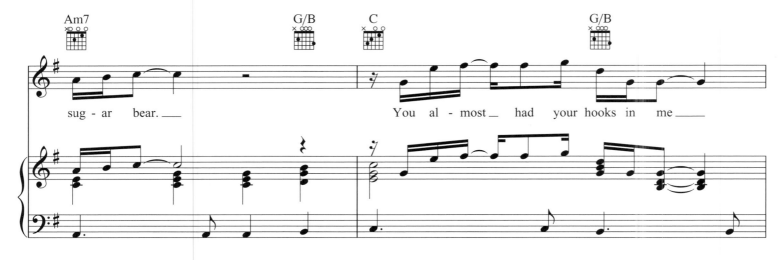

sug - ar bear. ___ You al - most ___ had your hooks in me ___

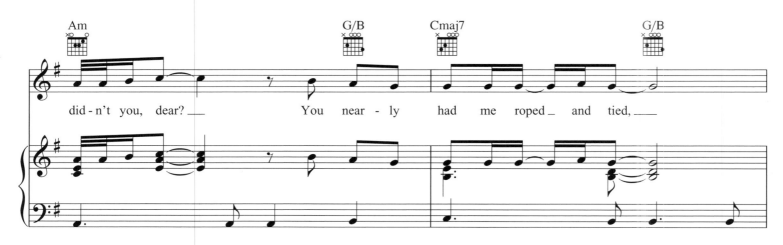

did - n't you, dear? ___ You near - ly had me roped ___ and tied, ___

al - tar bound, ___ hyp - no - tized, ___ sweet free - dom whis-pered in ___ my ear. ___ You're a

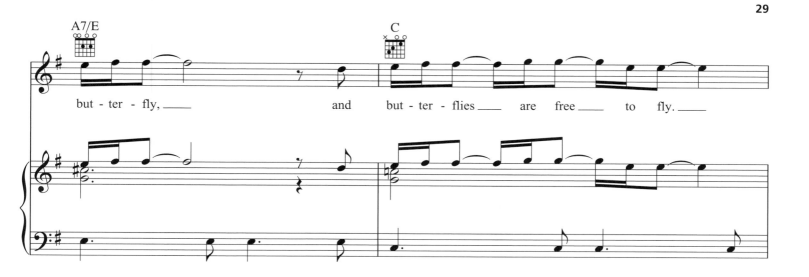

but - ter - fly, _____ and but - ter - flies _____ are free _____ to fly. _____

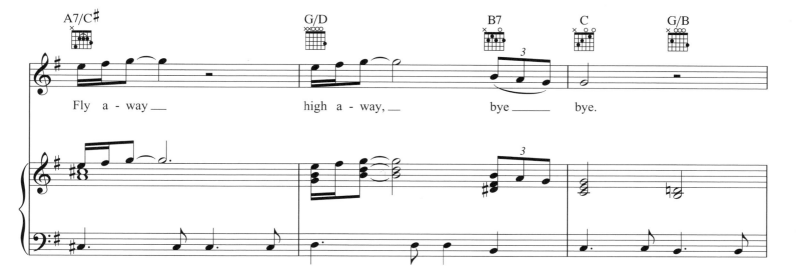

Fly a - way _____ high a - way, _____ bye _____ bye.

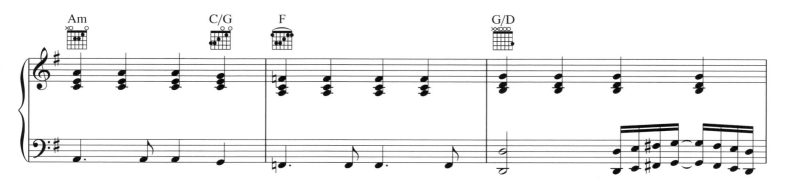

To Coda ✛

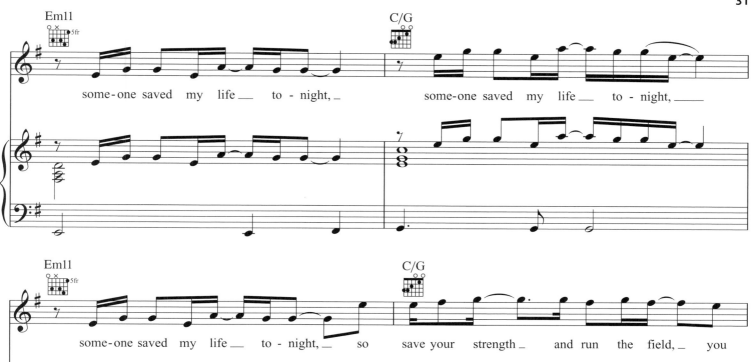

some-one saved my life __ to - night, __ some-one saved my life __ to - night, _____

some-one saved my life __ to - night, __ so save your strength __ and run the field, __ you

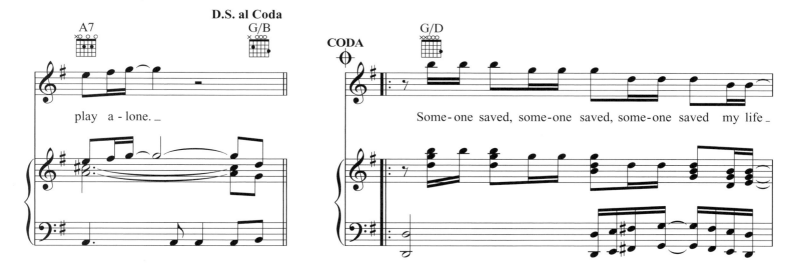

D.S. al Coda

play a - lone. __

CODA

Some-one saved, some-one saved, some-one saved my life __

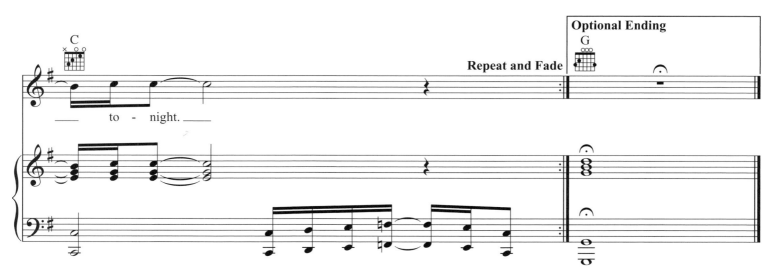

____ to - night. ____

Optional Ending

Repeat and Fade

TINY DANCER

Words and Music by ELTON JOHN
and BERNIE TAUPIN

(1., 3.) Blue - jean ba - by. ___ L. ___ A. ___ la - dy. ___
(2.) Je - sus freaks ___ out in ___ the ___ street ___

Seam-stress for ___ the band. ___
hand - ing tick - ets out ___ for God. ___

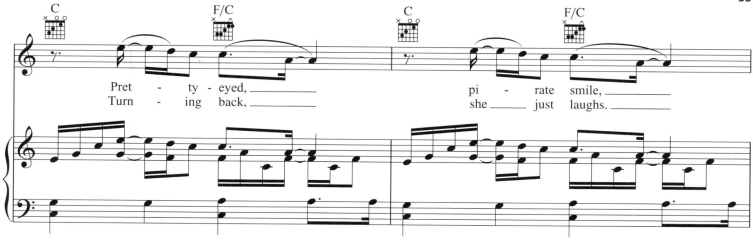

Pret - ty eyed, _____ pi - rate smile, _____
Turn - ing back, _____ she _____ just laughs. _____

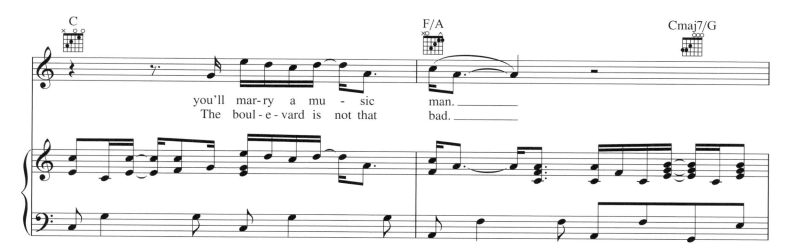

you'll mar - ry a mu - sic man. _____
The boul - e - vard is not that bad. _____

Bal - le - ri - na. You must ___ have seen _____ her
Pia - no ___ man, _____ he makes ___ his stand _____

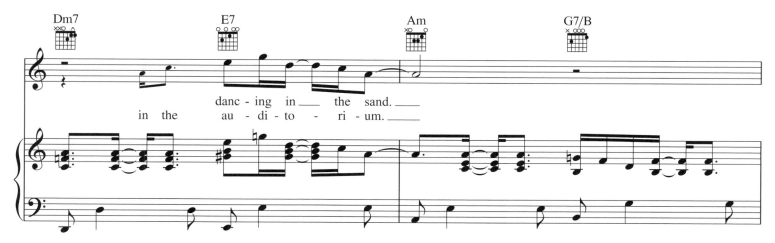

danc - ing in ___ the sand. _____
in the au - di - to - ri - um. _____

And now ____ she's in me, __ al - ways ___ with me, __
Look - ing on, _____ she sings the ___ songs. _____

ti - ny danc - er in my hand. _____
The word she ___ knows, the tune she hums. _____

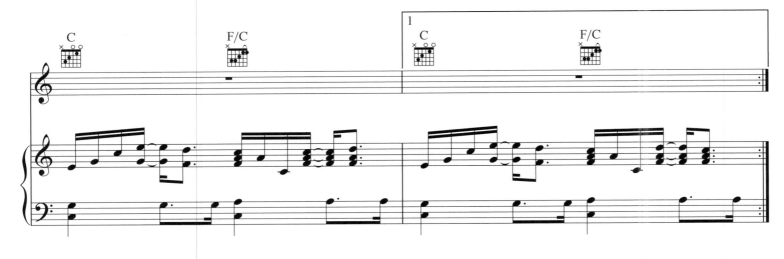

But, oh, how it feels ___ so real ___

ly - ing here with no one near. _ On - ly you, and you _ can

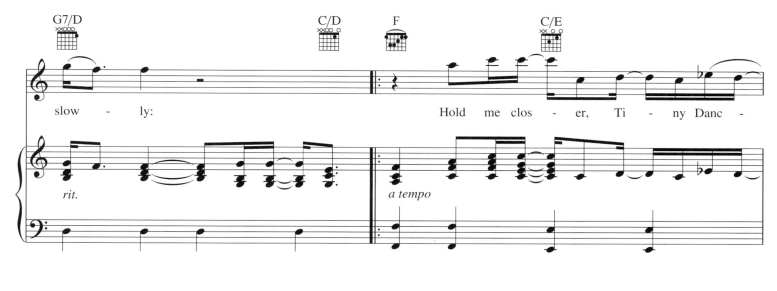

hear me when I _ say soft - ly,

slow - ly: Hold me clos - er, Ti - ny Danc -

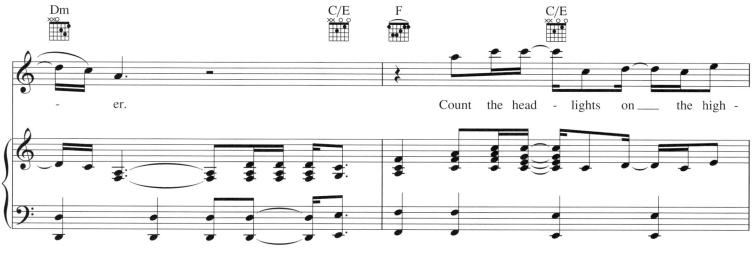

- er. Count the head - lights on _ the high -

way.

Lay me down _ in sheets _ of lin -

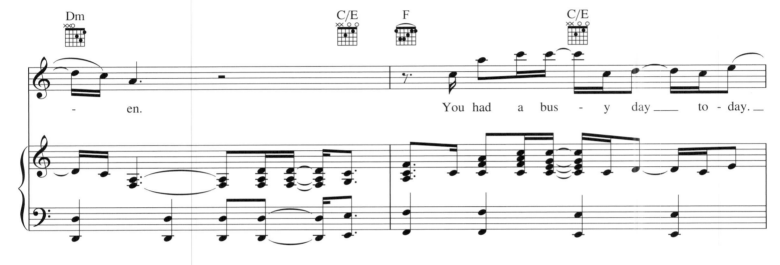

- en.

You had a bus - y day ___ to - day. _

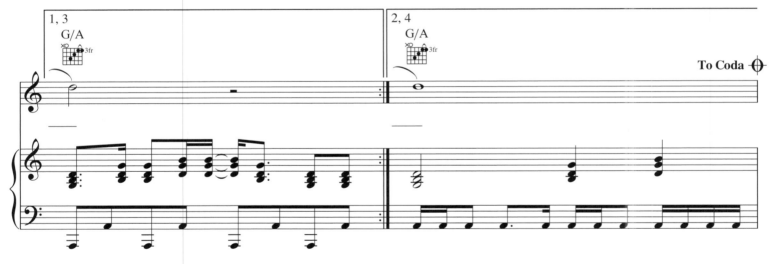

1, 3

2, 4

To Coda ⊕

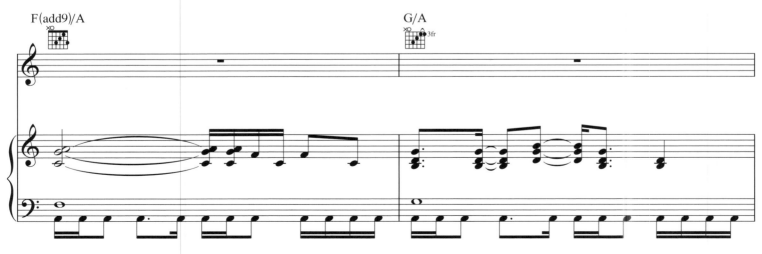

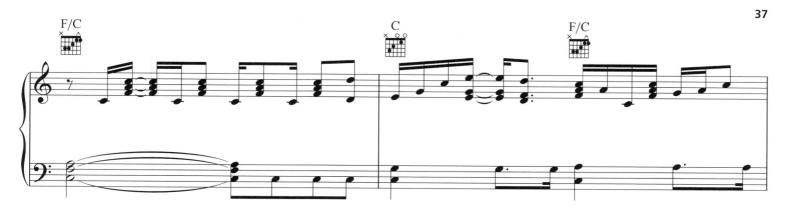

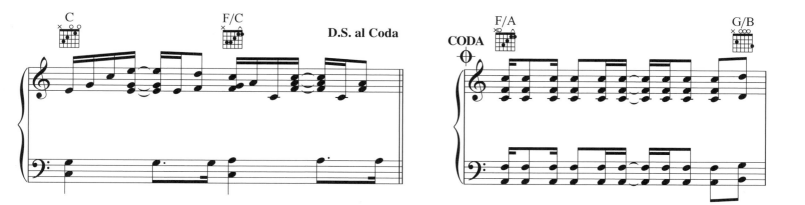

D.S. al Coda

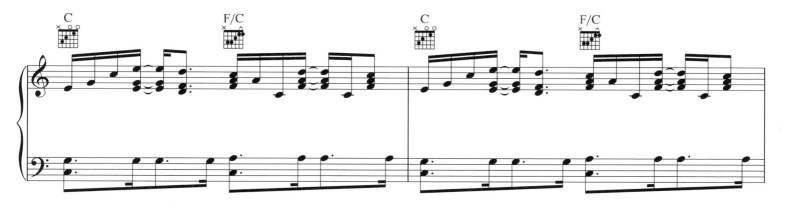

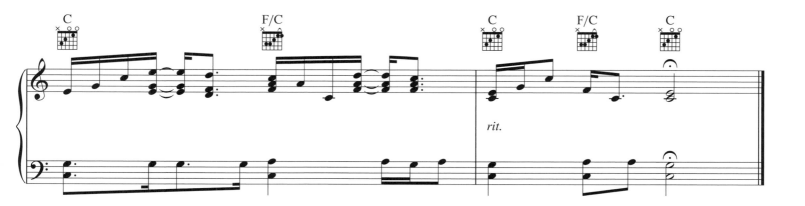

rit.

DON'T LET THE SUN
GO DOWN ON ME

Words and Music by ELTON JOHN
and BERNIE TAUPIN

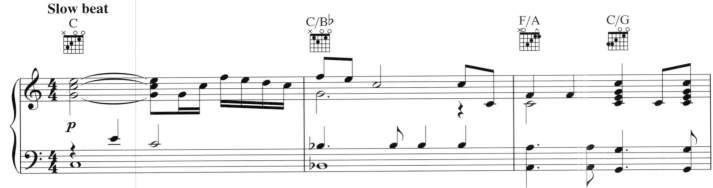

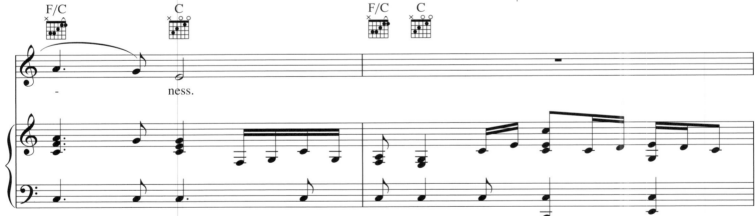

I'm __ grow-ing tired

and time stands still be - fore _____ me.

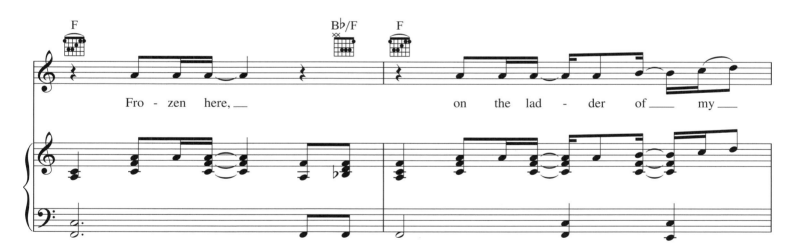

Fro - zen here, __ on the lad - der of __ my __

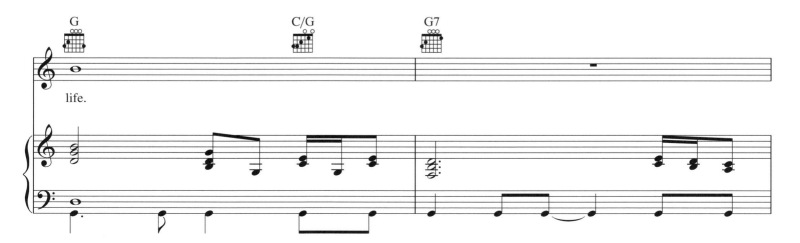

life.

Too late ___ to save my-self from fall - ing.

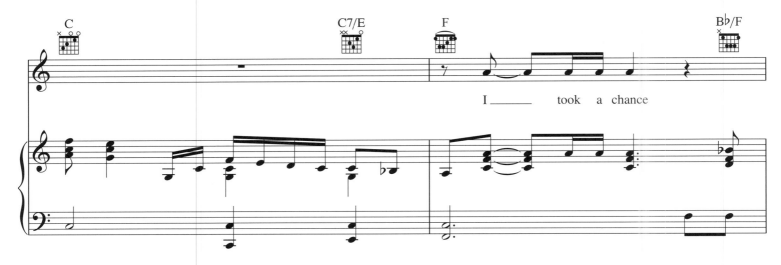

I ___ took a chance

and changed your way ___ of life. ___

But you mis-read my mean-ing when I met ___ you, ___

closed the door   and left me blind-

-ed _____ by _____ the light. _____

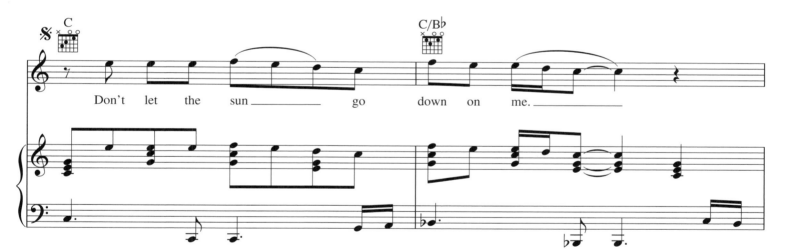

Don't let the sun _____ go down on me. _____

Al-though I _____ search my-self, it's al-ways some-one else I see. _____

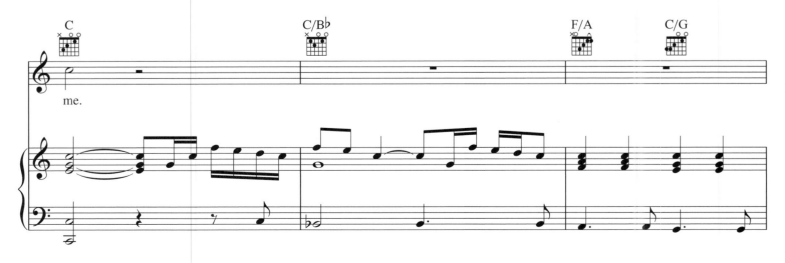

I can't find oh ___ the right ro -

man-tic line. ___ But see me once ___

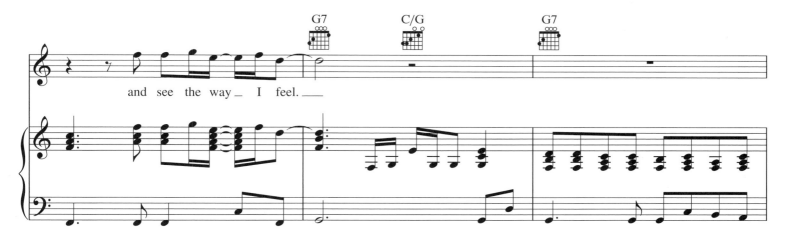

and see the way ___ I feel. ___

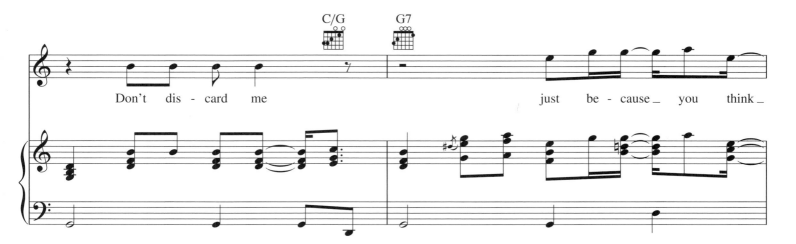

Don't dis - card me just be - cause ___ you think ___

I mean you harm.

But these cuts I have, oh, they need love to help them

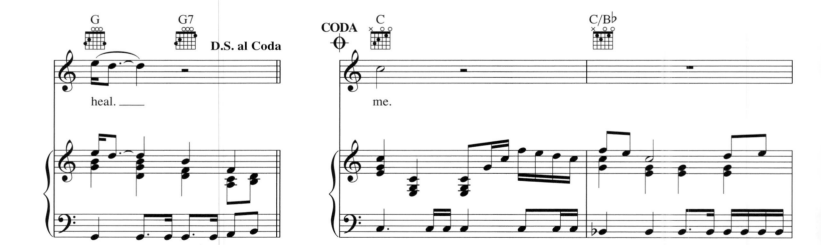

D.S. al Coda

heal.

CODA

me.

THE ULTIMATE SONGBOOKS

These great songbook/CD packs come with our standard arrangements for piano and voice with guitar chord frames plus a CD.
The CD includes a full performance of each song, as well as a second track without the piano part so you can play "lead" with the band!

1. Movie Music
Come What May • My Heart Will Go On (Love Theme from *Titanic*) • The Rainbow Connection • and more.
00311072 P/V/G.....................$14.95

2. Jazz Ballads
Georgia on My Mind • In a Sentimental Mood • The Nearness of You • The Very Thought of You • When Sunny Gets Blue • and more.
00311073 P/V/G.....................$14.95

3. Timeless Pop
Ebony and Ivory • Every Breath You Take • From a Distance • I Write the Songs • In My Room • Let It Be • Oh, Pretty Woman • We've Only Just Begun.
00311074 P/V/G.....................$14.95

4. Broadway Classics
Ain't Misbehavin' • Cabaret • If I Were a Bell • Memory • Oklahoma • Some Enchanted Evening • The Sound of Music • You'll Never Walk Alone.
00311075 P/V/G.....................$14.95

5. Disney
Beauty and the Beast • Can You Feel the Love Tonight • A Whole New World • You'll Be in My Heart • You've Got a Friend in Me • and more.
00311076 P/V/G.....................$14.95

6. Country Standards
Blue Eyes Crying in the Rain • Crazy • King of the Road • Oh, Lonesome Me • Ring of Fire • Tennessee Waltz • You Are My Sunshine • Your Cheatin' Heart.
00311077 P/V/G.....................$14.95

7. Love Songs
Can't Help Falling in Love • Here, There and Everywhere • How Deep Is Your Love • Maybe I'm Amazed • You Are So Beautiful • and more.
00311078 P/V/G.....................$14.95

8. Classical Themes
Can Can • Habanera • Humoresque • In the Hall of the Mountain King • Minuet in G Major • Symphony No. 5 in C Minor, 1st Movement Excerpt • and more.
00311079 Piano Solo.....................$14.95

9. Children's Songs
Do-Re-Mi • It's a Small World • Linus and Lucy • Sesame Street Theme • Sing • Winnie the Pooh • Won't You Be My Neighbor? • Yellow Submarine.
0311080 P/V/G.....................$14.95

10. Wedding Classics
Air on the G String • Ave Maria • Bridal Chorus • Canon in D • Jesu, Joy of Man's Desiring • Ode to Joy • Trumpet Voluntary • Wedding March.
00311081 Piano Solo.....................$14.95

11. Wedding Favorites
All I Ask of You • Don't Know Much • Endless Love • Grow Old with Me • In My Life • Longer • Wedding Processional • You and I.
00311097 P/V/G.....................$14.95

12. Christmas Favorites
Blue Christmas • The Christmas Song • Do You Hear What I Hear • Here Comes Santa Claus • Merry Christmas, Darling • Silver Bells • and more.
00311137 P/V/G.....................$15.95

13. Yuletide Favorites
Away in a Manger • Deck the Hall • The First Noel • Go, Tell It on the Mountain • Jingle Bells • Joy to the World • O Little Town of Bethlehem • and more.
00311138 P/V/G.....................$14.95

14. Pop Ballads
Have I Told You Lately • I'll Be There for You • Rainy Days and Monday • She's Got a Way • Your Song • and more.
00311145 P/V/G.....................$14.95

15. Favorite Standards
Call Me • The Girl from Ipanema • Moon River • My Way • Satin Doll • Smoke Gets in Your Eyes • Strangers in the Night • The Way You Look Tonight.
00311146 P/V/G.....................$14.95

16. TV Classics
The Brady Bunch • Green Acres Theme • Happy Days • Johnny's Theme • Love Boat Theme • Mister Ed • The Munsters Theme • Where Everybody Knows Your Name.
00311147 P/V/G.....................$14.95

17. Movie Favorites
Back to the Future • Theme from *E.T.* • Footloose • Somewhere in Time • Somewhere Out There • and more.
00311148 P/V/G.....................$14.95

18. Jazz Standards
All the Things You Are • Bluesette • Easy Living • I'll Remember April • Isn't It Romantic? • Stella by Starlight • Tangerine • Yesterdays.
00311149 P/V/G.....................$14.95

19. Contemporary Hits
Beautiful • Calling All Angels • Don't Know Why • If I Ain't Got You • 100 Years • This Love • A Thousand Miles • You Raise Me Up.
00311162 P/V/G.....................$14.95

20. R&B Ballads
After the Love Has Gone • All in Love Is Fair • Hello • I'll Be There • Let's Stay Together • Midnight Train to Georgia • Tell It like It Is • Three Times a Lady.
00311163 P/V/G.....................$14.95

21. Big Band
All or Nothing at All • Apple Honey • April in Paris • Cherokee • In the Mood • Opus One • Stardust • Stompin' at the Savoy.
00311164 P/V/G.....................$14.95

22. Rock Classics
Against All Odds • Bennie and the Jets • Come Sail Away • Do It Again • Free Bird • Jump • Wanted Dead or Alive • We Are the Champions.
00311165 P/V/G.....................$14.95

23. Worship Classics
Awesome God • Lord, Be Glorified • Lord, I Lift Your Name on High • Shine, Jesus, Shine • Step by Step • There Is a Redeemer • and more.
00311166 P/V/G.....................$14.95

24. Les Misérables
Bring Him Home • Castle on a Cloud • Empty Chairs at Empty Tables • I Dreamed a Dream • A Little Fall of Rain • On My Own • and more.
00311169 P/V/G.....................$14.95

25. The Sound of Music
Climb Ev'ry Mountain • Do-Re-Mi • Edelweiss • Maria • My Favorite Things • Sixteen Going on Seventeen • Something Good • The Sound of Music.
00311175 P/V/G.....................$15.99

26. Andrew Lloyd Webber Favorites
All I Ask of You • Amigos Para Siempre • As If We Never Said Goodbye • Everything's Alright • Memory • No Matter What • Tell Me on a Sunday • You Must Love Me.
00311178 P/V/G.....................$14.95

27. Andrew Lloyd Webber Greats
Don't Cry for Me Argentina • I Don't Know How to Love Him • The Phantom of the Opera • Whistle down the Wind • With One Look • and more.
00311179 P/V/G.....................$14.95

28. Lennon & McCartney
Eleanor Rigby • Hey Jude • The Long and Winding Road • Love Me Do • Lucy in the Sky with Diamonds • Nowhere Man • Strawberry Fields Forever • Yesterday.
00311180 P/V/G.....................$14.95

29. The Beach Boys
Barbara Ann • Be True to Your School • California Girls • Fun, Fun, Fun • Help Me Rhonda • I Get Around • Little Deuce Coupe • Wouldn't It Be Nice.
00311181 P/V/G.....................$14.95

30. Elton John
Candle in the Wind • Crocodile Rock • Daniel • Goodbye Yellow Brick Road • I Guess That's Why They Call It the Blues • Levon • Your Song • and more.
00311182 P/V/G.....................$14.95

31. Carpenters
(They Long to Be) Close to You • Only Yesterday • Rainy Days and Mondays • Top of the World • We've Only Just Begun • Yesterday Once More • and more.
00311183 P/V/G.....................$14.95

32. Bacharach & David
Alfie • Do You Know the Way to San Jose • The Look of Love • Raindrops Keep Fallin' on My Head • What the World Needs Now Is Love • and more.
00311218 P/V/G.....................$14.95

33. Peanuts™
Blue Charlie Brown • Charlie Brown Theme • The Great Pumpkin Waltz • Joe Cool • Linus and Lucy • Oh, Good Grief • Red Baron • You're in Love, Charlie Brown.
00311227 P/V/G.....................$14.95

34 Charlie Brown Christmas
Christmas Is Coming • The Christmas Song • Christmas Time Is Here • Linus and Lucy • My Little Drum • O Tannenbaum • Skating • What Child Is This.
00311228 P/V/G.....................$15.95

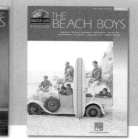
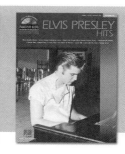

35. Elvis Presley Hits
Blue Suede Shoes • Can't Help Falling in Love • Heartbreak Hotel • Love Me • (Let Me Be Your) Teddy Bear and more.
00311230 P/V/G.................................$14.95

36. Elvis Presley Greats
All Shook Up • Don't • Jailhouse Rock • Love Me Tender • Loving You • Return to Sender • Too Much • Wooden Heart.
00311231 P/V/G.................................$14.95

37. Contemporary Christian
El Shaddai • Every Season • Here I Am • Jesus Will Still Be There • Let Us Pray • Place in This World • Who Am I • Wisdom.
00311232 P/V/G.................................$14.95

38. Duke Ellington Standards
Caravan • I Got It Bad and That Ain't Good • In a Sentimental Mood • Love You Madly • Mood Indigo • Sophisticated Lady • more.
00311233 P/V/G.................................$14.95

39. Duke Ellington Classics
Don't Get Around Much Anymore • I Let a Song Go out of My Heart • In a Mellow Tone • Satin Doll • Take the "A" Train • and more.
00311234 P/V/G.................................$14.95

40. Showtunes
The Best of Times • Hello, Dolly! • I'll Know • Mame • Summer Nights • Till There Was You • Tomorrow • What I Did for Love.
00311237 P/V/G.................................$14.95

41. Rodgers & Hammerstein
Bali Ha'i • Hello, Young Lovers • If I Loved You • It Might as Well Be Spring • Love, Look Away • Oh, What a Beautiful Mornin' • and more.
00311238 P/V/G.................................$14.95

42. Irving Berlin
Always • Blue Skies • Change Partners • Cheek to Cheek • Easter Parade • How Deep Is the Ocean (How High Is the Sky) • Puttin' on the Ritz • What'll I Do?
00311239 P/V/G.................................$14.95

43. Jerome Kern
Can't Help Lovin' Dat Man • A Fine Romance • I Won't Dance • I'm Old Fashioned • The Last Time I Saw Paris • Ol' Man River • and more.
00311240 P/V/G.................................$14.95

44. Frank Sinatra – Popular Hits
Come Fly with Me • Cycles • High Hopes • Love and Marriage • My Way • Strangers in the Night • (Love Is) The Tender Trap • Young at Heart.
00311277 P/V/G.................................$14.95

45. Frank Sinatra – Most Requested Songs
From Here to Eternity • I've Got the World on a String • Theme from "New York, New York" • Night and Day • Time After Time • Witchcraft • and more.
00311278 P/V/G.................................$14.95

46. Wicked
Dancing Through Life • Defying Gravity • For Good • I Couldn't Be Happier • I'm Not That Girl • Popular • What Is This Feeling? • The Wizard and I.
00311317 P/V/G.................................$15.99

47. Rent
I'll Cover You • Light My Candle • One Song Glory • Out Tonight • Rent • Seasons of Love • What You Own • Without You.
00311319 P/V/G.................................$14.95

48. Christmas Carols
God Rest Ye Merry, Gentlemen • Hark! the Herald Angels Sing • It Came upon the Midnight Clear • O Holy Night • Silent Night • What Child Is This? • and more.
00311332 P/V/G.................................$14.95

49. Holiday Hits
Frosty the Snow Man • Happy Xmas (War Is Over) • I'll Be Home for Christmas • Jingle-Bell Rock • Rudolph the Red-Nosed Reindeer • Santa Claus Is Comin' to Town • and more.
00311333 P/V/G.................................$14.95

50. Disney Classics
Some Day My Prince Will Come • When You Wish upon a Star • Whistle While You Work • Who's Afraid of the Big Bad Wolf? • Zip-A-Dee-Doo-Dah • and more.
00311417 P/V/G.................................$14.95

51. High School Musical
9 songs, including: Breaking Free • Get'cha Head in the Game • Start of Something New • We're All in This Together • What I've Been Looking For • and more.
00311421 P/V/G.................................$19.95

52. Andrew Lloyd Webber Classics
Another Suitcase in Another Hall • Close Every Door • Love Changes Everything • The Perfect Year • Pie Jesu • Wishing You Were Somehow Here Again • and more.
00311422 P/V/G.................................$14.95

53. Grease
Beauty School Dropout • Grease • Greased Lightnin' • Hopelessly Devoted to You • Sandy • Summer Nights • You're the One That I Want • and more.
00311450 P/V/G.................................$14.95

54. Broadway Favorites
Big Spender • Comedy Tonight • Hello, Young Lovers • I've Grown Accustomed to Her Face • Just in Time • Make Someone Happy • My Ship • People.
00311451 P/V/G.................................$14.95

55. The 1940s
Come Rain or Come Shine • It Could Happen to You • Moonlight in Vermont • A Nightingale Sang in Berkeley Square • Route 66 • Sentimental Journey • and more.
00311453 P/V/G.................................$14.95

56. The 1950s
Blueberry Hill • Dream Lover • Fever • The Great Pretender • Kansas City • Memories Are Made of This • My Prayer • Put Your Head on My Shoulder.
00311459 P/V/G.................................$14.95

57. The 1960s
Beyond the Sea • Blue Velvet • California Dreamin' • Downtown • For Once in My Life • Let's Hang On • (Sittin' On) The Dock of the Bay • The Twist.
00311460 P/V/G.................................$14.99

58. The 1970s
Dust in the Wind • Everything Is Beautiful • How Can You Mend a Broken Heart • I Feel the Earth Move • If • Joy to the World • My Eyes Adored You • You've Got a Friend.
00311461 P/V/G.................................$14.99

61. Billy Joel Favorites
And So It Goes • Baby Grand • It's Still Rock and Roll to Me • Leave a Tender Moment Alone • Piano Man • She's Always a Woman • Uptown Girl • You May Be Right.
00311464 P/V/G.................................$14.95

62. Billy Joel Hits
The Entertainer • Honesty • Just the Way You Are • The Longest Time • Lullabye (Goodnight, My Angel) • My Life • New York State of Mind • She's Got a Way.
00311465 P/V/G.................................$14.95

63. High School Musical 2
All for One • Everyday • Fabulous • Gotta Go My Own Way • I Don't Dance • What Time Is It • Work This Out • You Are the Music in Me.
00311470 P/V/G.................................$19.95

64. God Bless America
America • America, the Beautiful • Anchors Aweigh • Battle Hymn of the Republic • God Bless America • This Is My Country • This Land Is Your Land • and more.
00311489 P/V/G.................................$14.95

65. Casting Crowns
Does Anybody Hear Her • East to West • Here I Go Again • Praise You in This Storm • Somewhere in the Middle • Voice of Truth • While You Were Sleeping • Who Am I.
00311494 P/V/G.................................$14.95

66. Hannah Montana
I Got Nerve • Just like You • Life's What You Make It • Nobody's Perfect • Old Blue Jeans • Pumpin' up the Party • Rock Star • We Got the Party.
00311772 P/V/G.................................$19.95

67. Broadway Gems
Getting to Know You • I Could Have Danced All Night • If I Were a Rich Man • It's a Lovely Day Today • September Song • The Song Is You • and more.
00311803 P/V/G.................................$14.99

68. Lennon & McCartney Favorites
All My Loving • The Fool on the Hill • A Hard Day's Night • Here, There and Everywhere • I Saw Her Standing There • Yellow Submarine • and more.
00311804 P/V/G.................................$14.95

69. Pirates of the Caribbean
All for One • Everyday • Fabulous • Gotta Go My Own Way • I Don't Dance • What Time Is It • Work This Out • You Are the Music in Me.
00311807 P/V/G.................................$14.95

70. "Tomorrow," "Put on a Happy Face," And Other Charles Strouse Hits
Born Too Late • A Lot of Livin' to Do • Night Song • Once upon a Time • Put on a Happy Face • Those Were the Days • Tomorrow • You've Got Possibilities.
00311821 P/V/G.................................$14.99

71. Rock Band
Black Hole Sun • Don't Fear the Reaper • Learn to Fly • Paranoid • Say It Ain't So • Suffragette City • Wanted Dead or Alive • Won't Get Fooled Again.
00311822 P/V/G.................................$14.99

72. High School Musical 3
Can I Have This Dance • High School Musical • I Want It All • A Night to Remember • Now or Never • Right Here Right Now • Scream • Walk Away.
00311826 P/V/G.................................$19.99

73. Mamma Mia! – The Movie
Dancing Queen • Gimme! Gimme! Gimme! (A Man After Midnight) • Honey, Honey • Lay All Your Love on Me • Mamma Mia • SOS • Take a Chance on Me • The Winner Takes It All.
00311831 P/V/G.................................$14.99

FOR MORE INFORMATION, SEE YOUR LOCAL MUSIC DEALER, OR WRITE TO:

HAL•LEONARD® CORPORATION
7777 W. BLUEMOUND RD. P.O. BOX 13819
MILWAUKEE, WISCONSIN 53213

Visit Hal Leonard Online at
www.halleonard.com

Prices, contents and availability subject to change without notice.

PEANUTS © United Feature Syndicate, Inc.

THE ULTIMATE SERIES

This comprehensive series features jumbo collections of piano/vocal arrangements with guitar chords. Each volume features an outstanding selection of your favorite songs. Collect them all for the ultimate music library!

Blues
90 blues classics, including: Boom Boom • Born Under a Bad Sign • Gee Baby, Ain't I Good to You • I Can't Quit You Baby • Pride and Joy • (They Call It) Stormy Monday • Sweet Home Chicago • Why I Sing the Blues • and more.
00310723 . . . . $19.95

Broadway Gold
100 show tunes: Beauty and the Beast • Do-Re-Mi • I Whistle a Happy Tune • The Lady Is a Tramp • Memory • My Funny Valentine • Oklahoma • Some Enchanted Evening • Summer Nights • Tomorrow • many more.
00361396 . . . . $21.95

Broadway Platinum
100 popular Broadway show tunes, featuring: Consider Yourself • Getting to Know You • Gigi • Do You Hear the People Sing • I'll Be Seeing You • My Favorite Things • People • She Loves Me • Try to Remember • Younger Than Springtime • many more.
00311496 . . . . $22.95

Children's Songbook
66 fun songs for kids: Alphabet Song • Be Our Guest • Bingo • The Brady Bunch • Do-Re-Mi • Hakuna Matata • It's a Small World • Kum Ba Yah • Sesame Street Theme • Tomorrow • Won't You Be My Neighbor? • and more.
00310690 . . . . $18.95

Christmas – Third Edition
Includes: Carol of the Bells • Deck the Hall • Frosty the Snow Man • Gesu Bambino • Good King Wenceslas • Jingle-Bell Rock • Joy to the World • Nuttin' for Christmas • O Holy Night • Rudolph the Red-Nosed Reindeer • Silent Night • What Child Is This? • and more.
00361399 . . . . $19.95

Classic Rock
70 rock classics in one great collection! Includes: Angie • Best of My Love • California Girls • Crazy Little Thing Called Love • Joy to the World • Landslide • Light My Fire • Livin' on a Prayer • (She's) Some Kind of Wonderful • Sultans of Swing • Sweet Emotion • and more.
00310962 . . . . $22.95

Classical Collection
Delightful piano solo arrangements, including: Air on the G String (Bach) • Für Elise (Beethoven) • Seguidilla from *Carmen* (Bizet) • Lullaby (Brahms) • Clair De Lune (Debussy) • The Swan (Saint-Saëns) • Ave Maria (Schubert) • Swan Lake (Tchaikovsky) • dozens more.
00311109 . . . . $17.95

Contemporary Christian
Includes over 40 favorites: Awesome God • Can't Live a Day • El Shaddai • Friends • God Is in Control • His Strength Is Perfect • I Can Only Imagine • One of These Days • Place in This World • and more.
00311224 . . . . $19.95

Country – Second Edition
90 of your favorite country hits: Boot Scootin' Boogie • Chattahoochie • Could I Have This Dance • Crazy • Down at the Twist And Shout • Hey, Good Lookin' • Lucille • When She Cries • and more.
00310036 . . . . $19.95

Gospel
Includes: El Shaddai • His Eye Is on the Sparrow • How Great Thou Art • Just a Closer Walk With Thee • Lead Me, Guide Me • (There'll Be) Peace in the Valley (For Me) • Precious Lord, Take My Hand • Wings of a Dove • and more.
00241009 . . . . $19.95

Jazz Standards
Over 100 great jazz favorites: Ain't Misbehavin' • All of Me • Come Rain or Come Shine • Here's That Rainy Day • I'll Take Romance • Imagination • Li'l Darlin' • Manhattan • Moonglow • Moonlight in Vermont • A Night in Tunisia • The Party's Over • Solitude • Star Dust • and more.
00361407 . . . . $19.95

Latin Songs
80 hot Latin favorites, including: Amapola (Pretty Little Poppy) • Amor • Bésame Mucho (Kiss Me Much) • Blame It on the Bossa Nova • Feelings (¿Dime?) • Malaguena • Mambo No. 5 • Perfidia • Slightly out of Tune (Desafinado) • What a Diff'rence a Day Made • and more.
00310689 . . . . $19.95

Love and Wedding Songbook
90 songs of devotion including: The Anniversary Waltz • Canon in D • Endless Love • Forever and Ever, Amen • Just the Way You Are • Love Me Tender • Sunrise, Sunset • Through the Years • Trumpet Voluntary • and more.
00361445 . . . . $19.95

Movie Music – Second Edition
73 favorites from the big screen, including: Can You Feel the Love Tonight • Chariots of Fire • Cruella De Vil • Driving Miss Daisy • Easter Parade • Forrest Gump • Moon River • That Thing You Do! • Viva Las Vegas • The Way We Were • When I Fall in Love • and more.
00310240 . . . . $19.95

New Age
Includes: Cast Your Fate to the Wind • Chariots of Fire • Cristofori's Dream • A Day Without Rain • The Memory of Trees • The Steamroller • and more.
00311160 . . . . $17.95

Nostalgia Songs
100 great favorites from yesteryear, such as: Ain't We Got Fun? • Alexander's Ragtime Band • Casey Jones • Chicago • Danny Boy • Second Hand Rose • Swanee • Toot, Toot, Tootsie! • 'Way Down Yonder in New Orleans • The Yellow Rose of Texas • You Made Me Love You • and more.
00310730 . . . . $17.95

Pop/Rock
70 of the most popular pop/rock hits of our time, including: Bad, Bad Leroy Brown • Bohemian Rhapsody • Dust in the Wind • Imagine • Invisible Touch • More Than Words • Smooth • Tears in Heaven • Thriller • Walking in Memphis • You Are So Beautiful • and more.
00310963 . . . . $22.95

Reggae
42 favorite reggae hits, including: Get Up Stand Up • I Need a Roof • Jamaica Nice • Legalize It • Miss Jamaica • Rivers of Babylon • Tomorrow People • Uptown Top Ranking • Train to Skaville • Try Jah Love • and more.
00311029 . . . . $18.95

Rock 'N' Roll
100 classics, including: All Shook Up • Bye Bye Love • Duke of Earl • Gloria • Hello Mary Lou • It's My Party • Johnny B. Goode • The Loco-Motion • Lollipop • Surfin' U.S.A. • The Twist • Wooly Bully • Yakety Yak • and more.
00361411 . . . . $21.95

Singalong!
100 of the best-loved popular songs ever: Beer Barrel Polka • Crying in the Chapel • Edelweiss • Feelings • Five Foot Two, Eyes of Blue • For Me and My Gal • Indiana • It's a Small World • Que Sera, Sera • This Land Is Your Land • When Irish Eyes Are Smiling • and more.
00361418 . . . . $18.95

Standard Ballads
91 mellow masterpieces, including: Angel Eyes • Body and Soul • Darn That Dream • Day By Day • Easy to Love • Mona Lisa • Moon River • My Funny Valentine • Smoke Gets in Your Eyes • When I Fall in Love • and more.
00310246 . . . . $19.99

Swing Standards
87 songs to get you swinging, including: Bandstand Boogie • Boogie Woogie Bugle Boy • Heart and Soul • How High the Moon • In the Mood • Moonglow • Satin Doll • Sentimental Journey • Witchcraft • and more.
00310245 . . . . $19.95

TV Themes
More than 90 themes from your favorite TV shows, including: The Addams Family Theme • Cleveland Rocks • Theme from Frasier • Happy Days • Love Boat Theme • Hey, Hey We're the Monkees • Nadia's Theme • Sesame Street Theme • Theme from Star Trek® • and more.
00310841 . . . . $19.95

Prices, contents, and availability subject to change without notice. Availability and pricing may vary outside the U.S.A.

FOR MORE INFORMATION, SEE YOUR LOCAL MUSIC DEALER, OR WRITE TO:

HAL•LEONARD®
CORPORATION
7777 W. BLUEMOUND RD. P.O. BOX 13819 MILWAUKEE, WI 53213

www.halleonard.com

0609